# Curtis Aikens

## A Family and Friends Cookbook

Prospective Press
Winston-Salem

# Prospective Press

1959 Peace Haven Rd, #246, Winston-Salem, NC 27106 U.S.A.
prospectivepress.com

Published in the United States of America by Prospective Press

 AND  TRADEMARKS

ABC Soup: A Family & Friends Cookbook
Copyright © Curtis G. Aikens Sr., 2015
All rights reserved

Author photo (page vi) copyright © Suze Gorman, 2015

Mr. Aikens's shoes photo (back cover) copyright © Prospective Press, 2015

Cover and interior design © ARTE RAVE, 2015

Library of Congress Control Number 2015950317

ISBN 978-1-943419-05-0

Printed in the United States of America
First printing, December, 2015

1 3 5 7 9 10 8 6 4 2

The text of this book was typeset in Optima
Accent text was typeset in American Typewriter
The alphabet accent text was typeset in Phosphate

#### PUBLISHER'S NOTE

The information in this book is presented for entertainment purposes only and should not be construed as health advice or treatment. The publisher has neither tested, nor intends to test, the instructions or recipes in this book and makes no warranties, express or implied, as to the accuracy of the information contained herein or its suitability for any purpose.

Elements of this book are fictional. The people, names, characters, locations, activities, and events portrayed or implied by this book are the product of the authors' imaginations or are used either fictitiously or with permission. Any other resemblance to actual people, locations, and events is strictly coincidental.

Without limiting the rights as reserved in the above copyright, no part of this publication may be reproduced, stored in or introduced into any retrieval system, or transmitted—by any means, in any form, electronic, mechanical, photocopying, recording, or otherwise—without the prior written permission of the publisher. Not only is such reproduction illegal and punishable by law, but it also hurts the author who toiled hard on the creation of this work and the publisher who brought it to the world. In the spirit of fair play, and to honor the labor and creativity of the author and photographers, we ask that you purchase only authorized electronic and paper editions of this work and refrain from participating in or encouraging piracy or electronic piracy of copyright-protected materials. Please give authors a break and don't steal this or any other work.

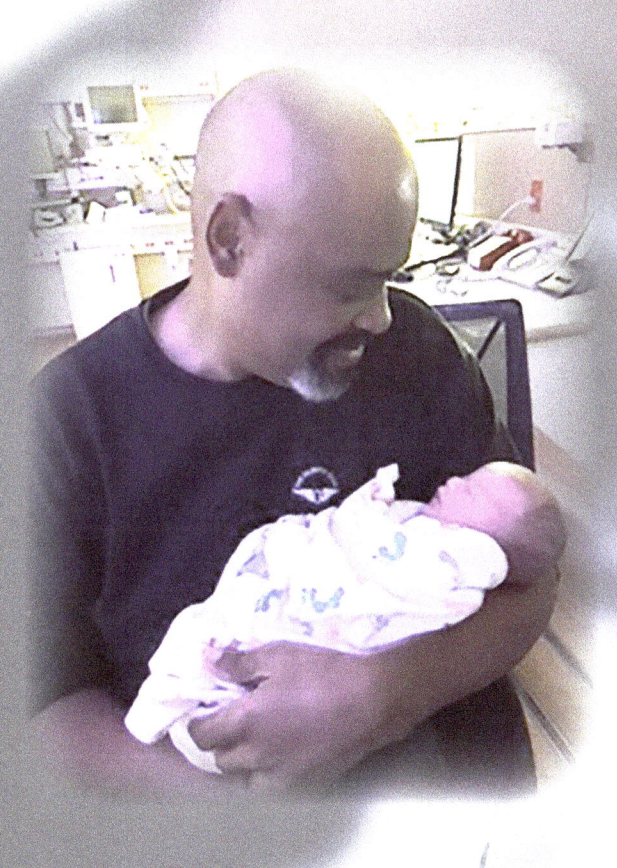

This book is dedicated to the kids.
Mine...
**Catherine Laura**,
**Curtis George Jr.**,
& **Cole Bennett**.
Also, the newest kid
in our family,
my grandson,
**Maverick Nathan Kapus**.

And your kids,
or you kids...
I love you all, 4 reals!

It is also to the young **Me**
in third grade
when I realized
I could not read.

I can do all things through
**Christ**
who strengthens me!

Spread Love!

**Mom** & **Dad**,
thank you...

# Hey, Everyone!

**I'm Chef Curtis,** and I love to cook and write books and help people learn about how to read. So when the publisher first talked with me about writing this book, I thought:

> "Yes, cool! I'll just dig up my trusty recipe that I have prepared **a hundred times:**
> **A** is for **ASPARAGUS,** the 1st ingredient in the soup,
> **B** is for **BROCCOLI...**
> ...oh, history! President **Bush** may not care for this vegetable, but a whole lot of folks who voted for him do! Therefore, broccoli will be #2 to hit the stew."

{ By the way, I am talking about **George H. Bush** our 41st President. He served right after **Ronald Regan** and just before **Bill Clinton**. Two elections later, President B's son, **George W. Bush**, won a very controversial (do you know that word?) election race against the sitting vice president, **Al Gore**! }

Sometimes, I get side tracked when telling a story, but I try not to get lost!

**You better be laughing!**

Kidding! Any-whoo...

1

What a fun recipe the original ABC Soup was. It had **eggplant**, **lemon grass**, and **okra**, plus all kinds of fun stuff from back in the day. Well the **days**, that is, like back when I had hair and a few more pounds around my middle...

There is this saying:

*"Never trust a skinny cook."*

It's an **old** saying! A bit later,* I'll talk more about the saying and how I **now** live and cook (*in this book and in some of my other books, if you all like this one).

Problem was, I couldn't find the recipe! I dug through files and boxes, I searched my computers, and I called friends, but I still couldn't find it. So I started dreaming about a new **ABC Soup...a neighborhood of soup.**

When I was a little boy—well, **young** boy, because I have always been **BIGGER** than most, hmm?—I spent a lot of time with all of my neighborhood friends:

**Jeffery**, my older brother;

**Ran** (**Randolph Camp**) my Best Bud;

His brother **Steve**;

Jeff's best friend, **Billy Boy** (**Raymond Carr, Jr.**);

Jeffery and Steve's other best friend (can't forget **Kookie!**);

**Bryan**, Billy's little brother, as well as my and Ran's other best friend!

Best Friends are like **LOVE**—you can never have too many of the one or too much of the other! So what do my **BEST FRIENDS** have to do with Soup or the **ABCs?** I wanted to start this book by talking about the fellas I grew up with—the fellas from my neighborhood (and there were other best friends...I'm trying to figure out a way to talk about them too, LOL!)—because **BEST FRIENDS** and using the **ABCs** to make a **SOUP** *could* be a pretty good metaphor.

{ Do you know the definition of the word "metaphor"? If not, no worries...I'll share the meaning with you at the end of the book. Promise. But let's see if you can figure it out first. }

I just love **Aa Bb Cc Dd Ee Ff Gg Hh Ii Jj Kk Ll Mm Nn Oo Pp Qq Rr Ss Tt Uu Vv Ww Xx Yy Zz** because they are friends and neighbors...can you see that? I love all 26 households of this neighborhood—let's call it *Alphabet Street!*—because every word I can think, say, write, or use starts with, ends with, and in the middle (if needed) is filled with letters from this little street! I think that is so cool!

Just like when I was a kid, I can still have lots of fun even being by myself. Oh yeah, I loved playing by myself—one of my other best friends is...**ME!** What? You were thinking that too, right? Here is a poem I wrote. Read it, think about it (grownups say *"reflecting"* when they mean *"thinking about it"*), and then read it again, out loud, to a friend. If you are by yourself, remember that you're never really alone when you can connect with your best friend—

right inside of you! And if you are by yourself, read the poem while looking in the mirror, then you'll really be **reflecting!**

**ME, I, YOU, AND**

I LOVE BEING ME.
WHY NOT?
AFTER ALL, I AM ALL I'VE GOT.
I LOVE LEARNING ABOUT ME,
IN HOPES TO BE BETTER FOR AND TO YOU.
WHEN I CAN LISTEN, REALLY LISTEN,
I HEAR YOU IN ME...AND, ME IN YOU.
—CURTIS GEORGE AIKENS, SR.
MAY, 2014

Reflect. Now please read it again.

What does my **little poem** cause you to **think** and **feel?** Remember, I would love to hear from you, or you can talk with a family member, a friend, or your teacher about your feelings and thoughts. How do you feel about A, B, and C, and all their friends, or as they are collectively known, **the Alphabet?** Please tell me. You can write me; just address your letter to:

CHEF CURTIS
PO BOX 575
CONYERS, GA
30012

*Who knows, I might send you something back. Wouldn't that be nice?*

So this book: **The Families, The Friends, THE Alphabet Soup Neighborhood Soup Cookbook,** is your guide to the soups from **Families A** to **Z**, as well as my one big **COMMUNITY SOUP** using all the letters of the Alphabet Community.

## Let's Get Started!

Twenty-six families live in this HOOD—**Family A** through **Family Z**. And in just about every house, they make soup every day, featuring a vegetable that starts with the single letter on the mail box out front. Each family is so proud of their soups. **Family A** makes the bomb Asparagus Soup, and their Artichoke Soup is equally EXPLOSIVE! At the house of **Family P**, the Pumpkin Soup is to LIVE for, while **Family T's** Tomato Soups are WORLD RENOWNED! **Family K** makes Kohlrabi Soup; you know about this vegetable, right?

Our tour of the neighborhood begins with **Family A**. And A is for ASPARAGUS, the 1st ingredient of the **COMMUNITY SOUP**. This vegetable is outstanding! If you haven't yet had asparagus, what are you waiting for?

**Turn the page...**

# A is for ASPARAGUS SOUP

**Family A** is so excited about their asparagus this year because the seeds were planted three-years ago and it takes that long before the vegetable has matured enough to be harvested. Asparagus spears will grow larger each season for about 15 years. After that... well, the asparagus patch the family had been harvesting from is about 16-years old, and the vegetables are getting tired looking and don't taste as sweet. But **Father A** has a surprise for the family and the neighborhood: he planted some PURPLE asparagus!

Have you ever seen or tasted **purple** asparagus? I have and I love it! There is also a white asparagus, which is tasty. Now any color asparagus is great—the plant is one of my FAVORITE veggies—but the **purple** grass* just seems to have more of that great flavor!

*Grass is one of the names that produce people use for asparagus!

FOR COMMUNITY SOUP: ONE POUND OF ASPARAGUS CUT INTO 1-INCH PIECES.

## ingredients

| | | |
|---|---|---|
| 1 | pound | fresh asparagus, green or purple |
| ¾ | cup | chopped onion |
| ½ | cup | vegetable broth |
| 1 | tablespoon | butter |
| 2 | tablespoons | all-purpose flour |
| 1 | teaspoon | salt |
| 1 | pinch | ground black pepper |
| 1¼ | cups | vegetable broth |
| 1 | cup | milk |
| ½ | cup | yogurt |
| 1 | teaspoon | lemon juice |
| ¼ | cup | grated Parmesan cheese |

## method

- Place the asparagus and onion in a saucepan with ½ cup vegetable broth. Bring the broth to a boil, reduce heat, and let simmer until the vegetables are tender.
- Reserve a few asparagus tips for garnish. Place remaining vegetable mixture in an electric blender and purée until smooth.
- Melt butter in the pan that had been used for simmering the asparagus and onions. Stir, while sprinkling flour, salt, and pepper into the butter. Do not let the flour brown. Allow the mixture to cook for only 2 minutes.
- Stir in remaining 1¼ cups vegetable broth and raise the heat, stirring until it comes to a boil.
- Stir the vegetable purée and milk into the saucepan. Whisk yogurt into the mixture, followed by lemon juice. Stir the soup until heated through, and then ladle into bowls.
- Garnish with reserved asparagus tips, and sprinkle with Parmesan cheese, if desired.

# B is for BROCCOLI SOUP

**Broccoli!** My kids called it baby trees, because I would cut and trim the stalks and florets to make the vegetable more appealing for the little ones. It worked. Years ago, before you were born, the first **President Bush** caused a big stink by saying he did not like broccoli. WOW! Farmers all across the country were a little upset, but the President's wife, the **First Lady of Family B, Mrs. Barbara Bush** (what a sweet person), saved the day by sharing with the country how much she enjoyed the vegetable, and she got her husband off the hook!

Me and Curtis Junior at the White House with Mrs. Bush.

The First Lady invited me to the White House because she and I had more in common than our love of Broccoli—we both work hard to help people who cannot read get into reading programs. Kids and grownups alike!

I love you, Mrs. Barbara Bush!

FOR COMMUNITY SOUP: ONE POUND OF BROCCOLI FLORETS, TRIMMED.

## ingredients

| | | |
|---|---|---|
| 4 | tablespoons | butter, room temperature |
| 1½ | pounds | fresh broccoli |
| 1 | large | onion, chopped |
| 1 | large | carrot, chopped |
| 3 | tablespoons | all-purpose flour |
| 1 | teaspoon | salt |
| 4 | cups | vegetable broth, low sodium |
| ½ | cup | cream |

Salt and freshly ground black pepper, to taste.

## method

- Melt 4 tablespoons of butter in a heavy, medium-sized pot over medium-high heat.
- Add broccoli, onion, carrot, salt, and pepper, and sauté until the onion is translucent—about 6 minutes.
- Add the flour, and cook for 1 minute—until the flour reaches a blond color. Add broth and bring to boil.
- Simmer uncovered until the broccoli is tender—about 15 minutes. Pour in cream. With an immersion blender, purée the soup.
- Add salt and pepper to taste. Enjoy!

# C is for CARROT SOUP

**Family C** is so proud of their **Carrot Soup!** Whenever they are having company, this is the soup **Poppa C** asks **Mama C** to prepare. Not just because **Mama C** makes the **Greatest Carrot Soup** in the world, according to **Pops**, but he also gets to brag and tell everyone that carrots are one of the oldest and most healthy vegetables ever! They're loaded with **Vitamin A**, a fact he is glad to share with **Mr. A** two doors away.

You should hear **Mr. C**, he sounds like one of those TV pitch men, pushing the stuff on a late-night infomercial: "The carrot is a real Super Food, one carrot has only about 25 calories, and provides six grams of carbohydrates, exactly the amount the brain needs to function every hour! It's low in calories, and high in flavor and riboflavin. Plus, the carrot is a good source of fiber," he adds with a little smile. "Fiber! It keeps things moving through the body!" That **Mr. C!** Don't get him started on **celery**, which is the vegetable the family takes to the community soup gathering.

FOR COMMUNITY SOUP: ONE OR TWO BUNCHES OF CELERY, WASHED AND CUT INTO 1-INCH PIECES.

## ingredients

| | | |
|---|---|---|
| 2-3 | tablespoons | oil |
| 2 | pounds | carrots, peeled & thinly sliced |
| 1 | large | sweet onion, chopped |
| 2 | cups | vegetable broth |
| 2 | teaspoons | cornstarch |
| 2 | tablespoons | tarragon, chopped |

Salt and freshly ground pepper to taste.
Toast points (slices of toast cut into triangles).

## method

- Heat oil in a large, heavy soup pot over medium-low heat and add the onion. Sauté about 7 minutes or until the onion starts to darken to a pretty brown—this shows that the sugar is being released from the vegetable.
- Add the carrots and ½ teaspoon of salt, cover partially, and cook for another 10 minutes, stirring often, until the vegetables are tender.
- Add broth, cornstarch, and salt (about 1½ teaspoons). Bring to a boil, reduce the heat, cover, and simmer 30 minutes, or until the carrots are tender.
- Blend the soup, either with a hand blender or in batches in a regular blender, and then strain the soup and return it to the pot. Stir and taste. Adjust seasoning, add pepper to taste, and heat through.
- Spoon in serving bowls, add toast point and herbs, and enjoy!

#  is for

On **Alphabet Street** tonight, at the home of **Family D**, dinner is **DAIKON SOUP!** Daikon (a **Japanese** word that means "Big Root") is a type of radish. One could call it a **GIANT** radish because, if allowed to, it can grow to weigh as much as 100 pounds! That's **BIG!** However, most daikon are picked when they are between 1 and 5 pounds.

While they eat, **Family D** loves to listen to Jazz, and one of their favorite groups is the world-renowned band, **Hiroshima!**

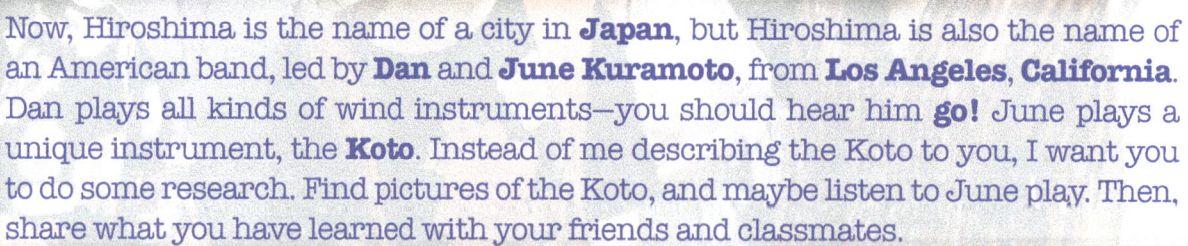

Now, Hiroshima is the name of a city in **Japan**, but Hiroshima is also the name of an American band, led by **Dan** and **June Kuramoto**, from **Los Angeles**, **California**. Dan plays all kinds of wind instruments—you should hear him **go!** June plays a unique instrument, the **Koto**. Instead of me describing the Koto to you, I want you to do some research. Find pictures of the Koto, and maybe listen to June play. Then, share what you have learned with your friends and classmates.

Hiroshima has been making Wonder-filled music for decades. Maybe, just maybe, I can talk June and Dan into coming with me to visit your school. Y'all will have to do your part by studying and writing! Send me a note telling me why we should come to your school. And tell me how daikon tastes to you. **Come on and try it!**

FOR COMMUNITY SOUP: TWO POUNDS OF DAIKON, PEELED & DICED.

## ingredients

| | | |
|---|---|---|
| 3 | medium | shitake mushrooms |
| 4 | medium | dry porcini mushrooms |
| 2 | tablespoons | vegetable oil |
| ½ | small | onion, thinly sliced |
| 1 | clove | garlic, finely chopped |
| 1¼ | cup | red grape juice* |
| 4 | cups | water |
| 1 | piece | kombu (seaweed), rinsed |
| 8 | ounces | white & brown mushrooms |
| ¼ | cup | soy sauce |
| ¾ | cup | daikon, peeled, & cubed |
| 1 | teaspoon | lime juice |

Add freshly ground black pepper & chopped chives for garnish.

*Because these recipes are for children to make and eat, I have substituted grape juice for the wine I would normally use.

## method

- Pre-soak the porcini mushrooms. Heat the oil in a medium saucepan over medium-low heat. Add the onion and sauté until translucent. Add the garlic and sauté, about 2 minutes. Add the grape juice, and cook until the volume is reduced by half.
- Add 4 cups water, plus the water from porcini mushrooms. Add the kombu, and bring the soup to a full boil, then reduce the heat to low, and remove and set aside the kombu.
- Slice the shitake mushrooms, and add them to the pan along with the other fresh mushrooms and soy sauce. Cut kombu into bite-size pieces and return to pan. Add daikon and simmer until softened, about 3 to 5 minutes. Add some pepper and lime juice to taste.
- To serve, divide the soup among four pre-warmed soup bowls and garnish with chives. Enjoy!

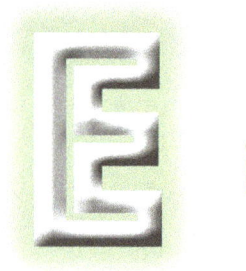 is for

**The Family E** got the idea for this soup—or should I say the inspiration came—while hanging out at the house of the **G's**. Here is the story...

**Family E** was visiting the **G's** one evening for dinner, and **Mr. and Mrs. G** served the most wonder-filled **Garlic Soup**. **Mr. E.** loved the soup so much that it was all he could do to keep from begging for the recipe. On the way home, **Mr. E** said to his wife, "Honey that soup was so **GOOD!** It's a shame garlic doesn't start with an E."

(Earlic.... that would not work!)

**Mrs. E**, one of the smartest people in the Alphabet community—holding several advanced degrees, and being both the author of four books and a certified culinary professional (do you know what that is?)—put her hand on her husband's cheek and said, in her calm, cool, and collected voice, "Darling, there's always Elephant Garlic."

I just love that story!
Elephant Garlic looks like regular garlic—only **supersized!** One would think its taste is super strong, but in reality elephant garlic has a milder flavor—a fact **Mrs. E** did not share with her husband.

FOR COMMUNITY SOUP: SEVEN CLOVES OF ELEPHANT GARLIC, PEELED AND CRUSHED.

## ingredients

| | | |
|---|---|---|
| 4 | tablespoons | vegetable oil |
| 2 | medium | leeks,* washed and sliced |
| 7 | cloves | elephant garlic, peeled, cubed |
| 3 | cups | vegetable broth |
| 2 | pounds | potatoes, peeled, cubed |
| 1 | tablespoon | salt |
| ¼ | teaspoon | ground black pepper |

* Wash leeks well and use only the white and light green portions.

## method

- Heat two tablespoons of oil in a heavy pot. When hot, add the leeks and garlic.
- Cook over medium heat for about 3 minutes, or until the vegetables begin to soften, add the broth, potatoes, and salt, and bring to a boil. Cover, reduce the heat, and boil gently for 25 minutes.
- If you like chunky soup, you can go ahead and dish it up, with a little buttered cornbread on the side. Or for smooth, creamy, chowder-like soup, strain the soup, purée the soft chunk vegetables, add the liquid, stir until smooth, and serve with that hot, buttered cornbread.

# F is for FAVA BEAN SOUP

**Daddy F**, loves **Fava Bean Soup** because, according to him, "It fills me up, from the top of my head to the bottom of my feet! And **Mama F**, you make great Fava Bean Soup!"

Speaking of **Europe**...I had always wanted to go. I finally got the chance, and one of the places I visited had great pizza and this tower. Where was I?

**Fava Beans** have several nicknames: Horse Bean, Faba Bean, and Board Bean—due to its wide flat seeds. The fava bean was the go to bean in Europe before those folks came to the new world and found all of the tasty pea varieties in the Americas.

I was in Pisa, Italy. That's their famous "Leaning Tower" behind me.

*For community soup: three cups of fava beans.*

## ingredients

| | | |
|---|---|---|
| 2 | cups | fava beans, fresh, shelled |
| 2 | tablespoons | olive oil |
| 2 | | leeks,* sliced |
| 2 | stalks | celery, sliced |
| 1 | large | onion, chopped |
| 2 | large | carrots, peeled, & diced |
| 2 | medium | turnips, peeled, & diced |
| 1 | small | potato, peeled, & diced |
| 2 | quarts | water or vegetable broth |
| ½ | teaspoon | white pepper, ground |
| ½ | teaspoon | turmeric |

For added flavor, make a bouquet garni by wrapping a couple of sprigs of parsley, a bay leaf, and several sprigs of cilantro into a cheese cloth bag. Then, tie it closed and add it to the soup when called for.

Salt to taste.

* Wash leeks well and use only the white and light green portions.

## method

- Heat one tablespoon of olive oil over medium heat in a large, heavy soup pot or Dutch oven and add the leeks, onion, carrots, and celery.
- Cook, while stirring, until vegetables are just tender, or about 7 minutes, and add the turnips, potatoes, fava beans, water or broth, salt, and the bouquet garni.
- Bring to a boil, reduce the heat, cover, and simmer for 45 minutes, or until the vegetables are very tender. Remove and discard the bouquet garni.
- Purée the soup using a hand blender. Add the pepper, turmeric, and chopped cilantro, and bring soup to a simmer over medium-low heat. Then, turn the heat to low, cover, and let it continue to simmer, stirring often, for 30 to 35 minutes.
- Taste, and adjust salt and pepper. Dish it up, and garnish with cilantro leaves and a drizzle of extra virgin olive oil over each serving.

 is for

Tonight, at the **G Family's** house, **Mr. G** is in charge of Grub (dinner), because **Mama G** is having a Girls Night Out Gathering at the Giants Game! Way to Go, **Mrs. G**! She is a big baseball fan, but **Mr. G** is always complaining about his stomach hurting when he eats too much ballpark food. So **Mrs. G** said, "Honey, stay home and make Ginger Soup, because ginger helps to settle an upset tummy!"

What do you know about ginger? Is it a plant? Is it a flower? Is it a root? It's all of those! Some of the best is grown in Hawaii—the roots* are sweet, the flowers are bold in color, and the plant is a strong green. Take a look!

Zingiber officinale

*Actually, the "roots" of the ginger plant are a type of underground stem called a "rhizome" (RYE-zohm).

FOR COMMUNITY SOUP: THREE TABLESPOONS OF CHOPPED GINGER.

## ingredients

| | | |
|---|---|---|
| 1 | tablespoon | canola oil |
| 1 | large | sweet onion, chopped |
| 1 | pound | butternut squash, peeled & diced |
| 2 | tablespoons | fresh ginger, peeled & minced |
| 1 | pound | sweet potatoes, peeled & diced |
| 1 | medium | yellow potato, peeled & diced |
| 6 | cups | vegetable broth |

Add salt and freshly ground pepper to taste.

## method

- Heat the oil in a heavy soup pot over medium heat. Add the onion and cook, stirring until tender—about 7 minutes. Add the ginger, and stir together for about 2 minutes.
- Add the squash, sweet potatoes, yellow potato, and broth, and bring to a boil. Add salt, and then reduce the heat, cover, and simmer 45 minutes or until all of the ingredients are thoroughly tender.
- Using an hand-held blender, purée the soup, and then stir with a whisk to even out the texture. Heat through, adjust the salt, and add pepper to taste.
- Serve and enjoy.

 is for **HORSERADISH SAUCE & HERB VEGETABLE SOUP**

**Mama H** is one creative cook! She has to be, because there aren't too many vegetables that start with the letter **H.** However, the group of seasoning plants called **herbs** is very large. For instance, at **Family T's** house, tonight's soup could feature **thyme**, which would mean that **Mrs. T** would get a double **T** bonus with **Thyme and Tomato Soup.** Whereas **Mrs. B** could do the same by making **Broccoli with Basil Broth** and earn a triple because of the **B** in broth.

What do you think of **Mama H's** creativity?  Please let me know; send me a letter!

Horseradish Sauce

3/4 cup prepared white horseradish

2 cups sour cream

1/4 cup fresh chives, chopped

3 teaspoons fresh lemon juice

**FOR COMMUNITY SOUP: A DOUBLE-BATCH OF HORSERADISH SAUCE.**

## ingredients

### Herb Vegetable Soup

| | | |
|---|---|---|
| 2 | tablespoons | fresh basil, chopped |
| 2 | tablespoons | fresh thyme, chopped |
| 1 | medium | bay leaf |
| 3 | tablespoons | oil |
| 2 | large | onions, peeled & chopped |
| 3 | stalks | celery, chopped |
| 3 | medium | carrots, peeled & sliced |
| ¾ | inch piece | fresh ginger, peeled & cut in thirds |
| 3 | cloves | garlic, peeled |
| 4 | cups | water |
| 2 | pounds | fresh tomatoes, sliced |
| 2 | medium | zucchini, sliced |
| 1 | pound | fresh spinach |
| 1 | large | potato, peeled & chopped |
| ¼ | cup | barley |
| 2 | teaspoons | salt |

Freshly ground pepper to taste.

## method

- Heat the oil in a large stockpot or Dutch oven over medium heat. Add the onions, celery, carrots, ginger, and garlic. Sauté until the onions begin to soften and turn translucent—about 7 minutes.
- Add the water, tomatoes, zucchini, spinach, potato, and barley. Raise the heat to high and bring the soup to a boil. Once it boils, lower the heat and add the salt, basil, thyme, bay leaf, and pepper.
- Simmer the soup, partially covered, for 30 to 40 minutes. Remove the ginger, garlic cloves, and bay leaf. Adjust the salt and pepper to taste.
- Ladle the soup into bowls and add about ¼ teaspoon of horseradish sauce to each bowl. You can also add a little sour cream, if your sauce is too spicy. Enjoy!

# I is for INDIAN PEA SOUP

Because there are not very many vegetables available in the United States that begin with their letter, the **Family I** has to be like **Leonardo da Vinci** and be inventive! The family has created soups with vegetables from other countries, like **India** and **Italy**. One night, **Mother I** might make **Italian Eggplant Stew** or an **Indian** dish, like tonight's thick and rich **Indian Pea Soup.**

### What a smart woman!

And speaking of smarts, I've been blessed to know many smart women in my life and career, but this sweet lady (in the photo) really took the gâteau! **Mrs. Julia Child** was intelligent, intriguing, imaginative, innovative, inimitable, and a great cook!

I had the honor of hosting one of Julia's 90th-birthday parties (yes, she had several that year!), this one was in Baltimore, Maryland. BTW, gâteau means cake in French. Now why would I be using a French word to talk about Mrs. Child?
Read about her life and see if you can find out!

FOR COMMUNITY SOUP: TWO CUPS OF FRESH INDIAN PEAS.

## ingredients

| | | |
|---|---|---|
| 1½ | cups | fresh green Indian peas, cooked |
| 2 | medium | potatoes, peeled & diced |
| 2 | medium | ripe red tomatoes, finely chopped |
| 1 | small | sweet onion, chopped |
| 1 | tablespoon | fresh ginger, minced |
| 3 | cloves | garlic, minced |
| 2 | | green chilies (sweet or heat) |
| ½ | teaspoon | turmeric |
| ½ | teaspoon | cumin |
| 1 | teaspoon | coriander |
| 1 | teaspoon | garam masala* |
| 2 | teaspoons** | vegetable oil |
| 3 | cups | vegetable broth |
| 2 | tablespoons | cilantro, chopped |

*Garam masala is a blend of spices. You'll have to write to me for my blend.

**Use more oil, if needed. We want to sauté the spices, not burn them.

## method

- In a large stock pot, heat the oil. Add the ginger, garlic, onions, chilies, and tomatoes. Sauté until the tomatoes and onions are softened—about 3 to 5 minutes.
- Add the turmeric powder, coriander powder, cumin, and garam masala. Next, add the peas and cook about 2 minutes, add the potatoes and the vegetable broth, and bring the soup to a boil. Allow it to boil for about 5 minutes, and then lower it to a simmer for 30 minutes or until the potatoes have softened but aren't mushy.
- Remove 3 or 4 pieces of potato, mash them, and return them to the pot to thicken the soup. Stir, and add the cilantro just before serving.

 is for

The **J Family** truly enjoys Jicama. And they love sharing their gumbo—a thick, stew-like soup—when they have company.

**Jicama** (HICK-ama) is a vegetable that grows in the tropics, and it is used very much like we use potatoes here in the United States. It can fried, baked, boiled, or broiled. However, it is a bit more watery and a littler sweeter, which makes it a great addition to a simple salad. Like everything on this street of food, you should try it!

Jicama in hand!

Chef getting silly with Jicama!

24

FOR COMMUNITY SOUP: THREE MEDIUM JICAMA, PEELED AND DICED.

## ingredients

| | | |
|---|---|---|
| 3 | tablespoons | oil |
| 3 | tablespoons | flour |
| 1 | medium | sweet onion, chopped |
| 1 | medium | red onion, chopped |
| 4 | medium | carrots, chopped |
| 3 | stalks | celery, chopped |
| 2 | cloves | garlic, diced |
| 2 | medium | jicama, peeled & cubed |
| 2 | cups | okra, sliced |
| 2 | pounds | heirloom tomatoes, chopped |
| 3 | cups | vegetable broth |
| 16 | ounces | red kidney beans |
| 1 | | bay leaf |
| 5 | ounces | Cajun seasoning, more as desired |
| 4 | | green onions, chopped |
| 2 | tablespoons | parsley, chopped |

Hot sauce to taste.

## method

- In a large stock pot, heat the oil, and then add flour to it, a tablespoon at the time. Stir and cook the flour in the oil until it is nicely brown—making your roux. Take your time, you don't want the flour to burn.
- Add the onions and cook them for 2 to 3 minutes. Add the celery and cook it for about 2 minutes. If the roux starts to dry out, add a tablespoon or more of the vegetable broth.
- Add the peppers and stir. Place a lid on the pot for about 2 minutes, and then add garlic, carrots, and jicama, and allow it to cook about 2 more minutes. Add the remaining ingredients except the parsley.
- Bring soup to a boil, and then lower the heat to a simmer. Your gumbo will be ready to enjoy in about half an hour! Add the parsley just before serving.

# K is for KOHLRABI & KALE SOUP

Tonight, the **K family** is doubling up the **K** vegetables with **Kohlrabi** and **Kale.** The first of these vegetables is sometimes called turnip cabbage (If you visit the **T family** on certain nights, they will serve a soup with this same vegetable…That's tricky, **Family T**). As you might imagine, kohlrabi has the shape of a turnip, but with the purple or green color of a cabbage. Unsurprisingly, kohlrabi is a member of the cabbage family and has a mild, sweet taste. And kale! The **K's** love kale, a super-healty, leafy green that is also a member of the cabbage family. It comes in a dozen different varieties, and the **K's** eat it raw and cooked.

I think you will enjoy kohlrabi, if you try it. Remember, it comes in two colors: purple and green!
And you know about kale, right? Have you ever made kale chips? You should invite me to cook at your school and we could make kale chips together!

FOR COMMUNITY SOUP: FOUR KOHLRABI, PEELED AND SLICED.

## ingredients

| 2 | tablespoons | canola oil |
| 1 | large | sweet onion, chopped |
| 2 | medium | leeks,* washed & sliced |
| 4 | medium | carrots, peeled & sliced |
| 4 | | kohlrabi, trimmed, peeled, & diced |
| 1 | bunch | dark kale, washed & chopped |
| 3 | | turnips, peeled & diced |
| 2 | medium | potatoes, peeled & diced |
| 2 | quarts | vegetable broth |

Salt and freshly ground pepper to taste

One bouquet garni—a bay leaf, about a dozen peppercorns, a tablespoon of chopped ginger, 2 sprigs each of fresh thyme and parsley, all wrapped and tied in cheese cloth.

* Wash leeks well and use only the white and light green portions.

## method

- Heat the canola oil over medium heat in a large, heavy soup pot. Add the onion and cook, stirring, until it begins to soften—about three minutes.
- Add the leeks and continue cooking, stirring often, until tender but not browned, or about five more minutes. Add the carrots, kohlrabi, kale, turnips, potatoes, and broth. Bring soup to a boil and add the bouquet. Taste the soup, and add salt, if needed.
- Reduce the heat, cover the soup, and let it simmer for one hour. Remove the cheesecloth bag and discard it. With a hand-held blender, blend the soup until it is smooth.
- Pour the soup through a strainer into a bowl, pressing the soup through the strainer with the back of a ladle or with a pestle. Return the soup to the pot and heat it thoroughly. Add freshly ground pepper and salt to taste. Serve and enjoy the soup.

# L is for LEMON CUCUMBER CHILLED SOUP

**Lemon Cucumber** is also known as **Apple Cucumber** because of their round shape. However, when it's ripe, this vegetable looks very much like a lemon. The **Family L** loves serving it in this chilled soup.

Do you know another name for chilled soup?

Gazpacho!

You know what else is chill?
Me, hanging with the **Buddha** in **San Diego, California**.
I like taking photos of myself with the Buddha because I used to look like him. LOL!
Can you find the photos of me with a Buddha belly?

San Diego, CA

FOR COMMUNITY SOUP: FOUR POUNDS OF LEMON CUCUMBER, DICED.

## ingredients

| | | |
|---|---|---|
| 3-4 | | lemon cukes, peeled & sliced thin |
| 2 | cups | vegetable broth, chilled |
| 2 | cups | plain yogurt, Greek style is the rave |
| 3 | | shallots, peeled & minced |
| 2 | tablespoons | red onion, finely chopped |
| 1 | cup | watercress, chopped |
| 1 | cup | dill, coarsely chopped |

Salt and freshly ground pepper to taste.

## method

- In a mixing bowl, mix the cucumber slices with about 1 teaspoon of salt, and refrigerate them for about twenty minutes. Add the broth, black pepper, yogurt, shallots, and watercress—if you like—and stir. Taste the soup and adjust the seasoning.
- Just before serving the soup, garnish with some dill.

# M is for MOREL & MORE MOREL & WILD RICE SOUP

**Mama M** loves making this soup for the family because she gets to use the family letter twice. When all the Mom's of the Alphabet Community get together, there is an unofficial tally of how many times during the previous week multiple family letters were used during dinner menus!

This recipe uses fresh and dry (they're rehydrated upon cooking) Morels; that's why I used the **Morel and More Morel** moniker (moniker is another word for "nickname"). I use the dried Morels because adding them gives the soup a big boost in flavor! The Morel is called a mushroom, but in reality it is more closely related to the truffle than to mushrooms. Remember that, because one day that fact might help you win on a TV game show.

FOR COMMUNITY SOUP: THE SAME AMOUNT OF PREPARED MUSHROOMS, DRY AND FRESH, TO ADD TO THE BROTH POT.

## ingredients

| | | |
|---|---|---|
| 1 | ounce | dried Morel mushrooms |
| 3 | cups | boiling water |
| 1 | pound | fresh Morel mushrooms |
| 3 | tablespoons | corn oil |
| 1 | large | sweet onion, chopped |
| 4 | | carrots, diced |
| 2 | ribs | celery, diced |
| ½ | cup | white mushrooms, thickly sliced |
| 3 | cloves | garlic, minced |
| 1 | cup | wild rice |
| 2 | quarts | vegetable broth |
| 1 | tablespoon | fresh peas (frozen okay) |

Salt and freshly ground pepper to taste.
A bouquet garni made with a bay leaf and a few sprigs each of thyme, parsley, and rosemary.

## method

- Place the dried morel mushrooms in a bowl and pour on the boiling water. Let them sit for 30 minutes. Set a strainer over a bowl and line it with cheesecloth. Lift the mushrooms from the water, and squeeze them over the strainer. Rinse them with several changes of water, and then squeeze out the water and set the Morels aside. Pour the water that was used to soak the Morels through the cheesecloth-lined strainer, and set this water aside.
- Heat the oil in a large, heavy soup pot on medium heat. Add the onion, carrot, and celery. Cook them, stirring often, until they just about tender—about five minutes. Add the sliced fresh mushrooms. Keep cooking and stirring, until the mushrooms are beginning to soften—about 5 minutes. Add the garlic. Continue to cook for about five minutes, or until the mixture is juicy and starts to smell good. Add the rehydrated Morels, the wild rice, bouquet garni, mushroom soaking liquid, and vegetable broth. Add salt, to taste.
- Bring to a boil, reduce the heat, cover and simmer one hour. Add the peas, and simmer another 10 minutes. Remove the bouquet garni, taste the soup, and adjust the salt. Add freshly ground pepper and serve.

# N is for NUTTY BUTTERNUT SQUASH SOUP

**Mother N** knows how much her kids and husband love the hard fruits otherwise known as NUTS! With that in mind, she can make one recipe in so many different ways just by changing the nut she uses. Switch cashews for almonds or pecans or any one of the variety of nuts, and it's a whole new soup! Her family is happy!

Now I call that being **creative.**

And speaking of creative...this is my niece, Chef Joy. She's one of the most creative people I know!

FOR COMMUNITY SOUP:
ONE TABLESPOON OF NUTMEG.

## ingredients

| | | |
|---|---|---|
| 4 | tablespoons | butter, unsalted |
| 1 | large | Vidalia or sweet onion, chopped |
| 1 | cup | raw cashews |
| 2 | cloves | garlic, minced |
| 2 | large | butternut squash, peeled & diced |
| 5 | cups | vegetable broth |
| 3 | tablespoons | fresh ginger, peeled & minced |
| 2 | teaspoons | ground cumin |
| 2 | teaspoons | ground coriander |
| 1 | teaspoon | curry power |
| 1 | teaspoon | ground turmeric |
| 1 | cup | coconut milk |
| 1 | sprig | fresh rosemary |

Kosher salt and freshly ground pepper to taste.

## method

- In a large stockpot, on medium-high heat, melt the butter. Add the onions and cook, stirring, until they begin to soften—about 5 minutes. Add the nuts (cashews) and cook, stirring, until the onions are translucent and the cashews have slightly browned—about 4 minutes. Stir in the garlic and cook for 30 seconds. Add the squash, broth, ginger, cumin, coriander, curry powder, and turmeric, and stir to combine.
- Taste the soup, add ground pepper to taste, and bring the soup to a simmer (salt is always optional; we can train ourselves to require less salt. Remember, it is in everything already).
- Lower heat to a simmer, cover the pot, and simmer the soup until the squash is soft, or 20 to 25 minutes. Uncover the soup and let it cool for 15 minutes.
- With hand-held blender, purée the soup in the soup pot. Add the coconut milk and rosemary sprig, and cook over low heat, covered, until slightly thickened—about 15 to 20 minutes. Serve.

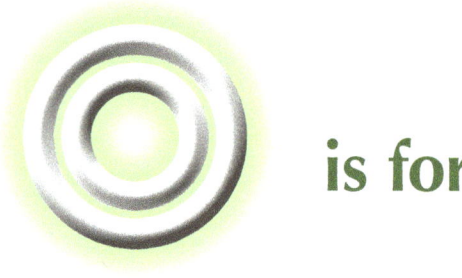

# O is for ONION SOUP SWEET VIDALIA

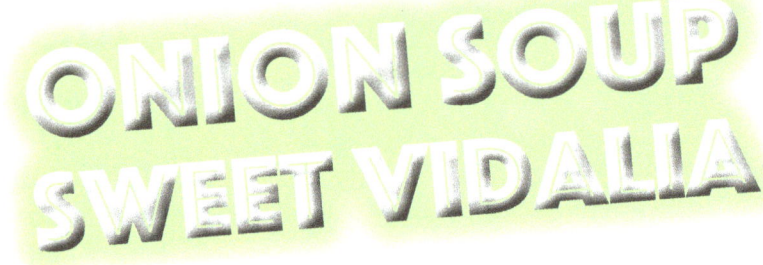

The **O family** got this recipe from me, **Chef Curtis G. Aikens Sr.**, I am proud to say. The **Vidalia Onion** is a sweet onion that is grown in the middle region of my home state of **Georgia**.

An old trick in buying onions is...

"The flatter the onion, the milder (sweeter) the taste."

Be sweet, spread love!

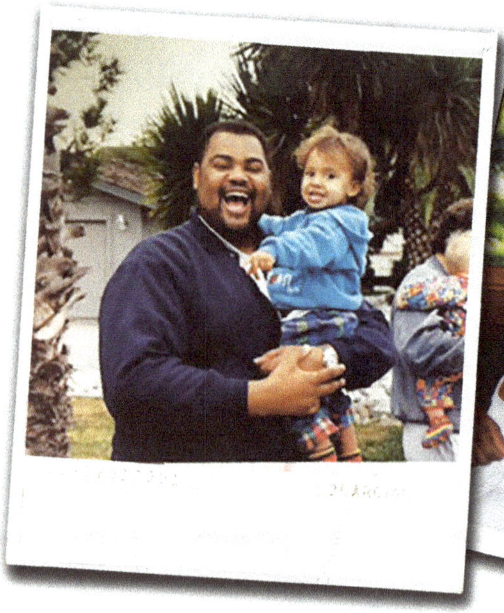

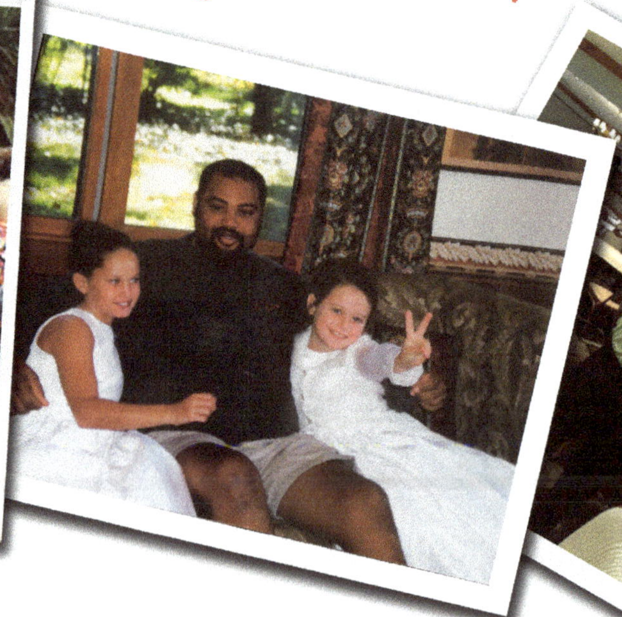

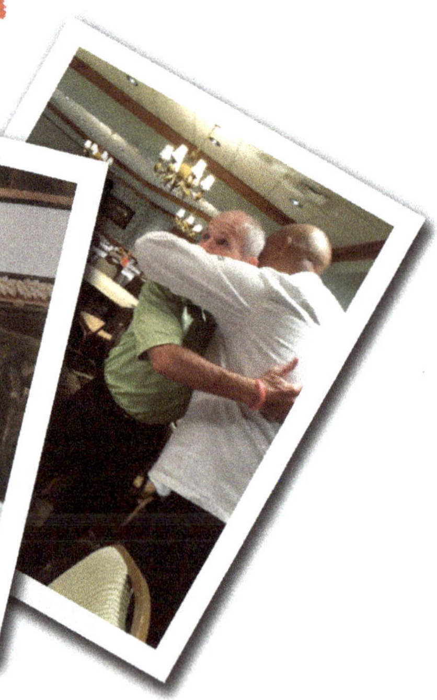

FOR COMMUNITY SOUP: THREE POUNDS OF VIDALIA ONIONS, CHOPPED AND SAUTÉED IN OIL UNTIL THEY ARE TRANSLUCENT.

## ingredients

| | | |
|---|---|---|
| 4 | large | Vidalia onions, peeled & sliced |
| 1 | tablespoon | butter |
| 3 | tablespoons | peanut oil |
| 4 | cups | vegetable broth |
| 1 | cup | white grape juice |
| 2 | tablespoons | chopped mixed herbs, such as chives, thyme, rosemary, sage, or tarragon |

Salt and freshly ground pepper to taste.
Serve with cornbread and cheddar cheese.

## method

- In a large stock pot, heat oil. Add the butter, and once it starts to melt, add the onion. Sauté the onion until it starts to brown. If the onion starts to dry out or stick to the pot, add some broth; you want the onion to brown nicely.
- Add the grape juice, broth, and herbs. Bring the soup to a boil, and then lower the heat and let simmer for about 35-40 minutes.
- Top slices of cornbread with cheese and place them in your bowls, add the hot soup, and then serve and enjoy.

 is for

The kids of **Family P** love **Pumpkin Soup** nights, because **Mam P** and **Dad P** allow the kids to pick a smaller pumpkin to carve into a **Jack-O'-Lantern** that gets to sit at the table at dinner!

Would you send me a picture of your next carved pumpkin? Do you know a pumpkin is a type of squash? Yes, it is. Write to me and tell me what other types of squash you like.

Here I am, sittin' and chillin' in **NYC** with some future **Jack-O'-Lanterns**. Can you guess what type of food is made by the restaurant I'm at? Look at the colors on the chair for a hint.

And there I am, sittin' and chillin' with my older son, Curtis Junior on Halloween, many years ago. He's grown since page 8!

FOR COMMUNITY SOUP: PEPPERS, HOT ONES, SLICED UP FOR THOSE WHO WANT TO SPICE UP THEIR SOUP!

## ingredients

| | | |
|---|---|---|
| 1 | medium* | pumpkin, cleaned out** |
| ½ | pound | sugar pumpkin, cubed |
| 2 | tablespoons | butter, melted |
| 2 | tablespoons | oil |
| 1 | large | onion, chopped |
| 3 | | carrots, chopped |
| 3 | ribs | celery, chopped |
| 4 | cups | vegetable broth |
| 1 | pound | fresh tomatoes, chopped |
| ½ | cup | rice |
| 2 | tablespoons | oregano |
| 2 | tablespoons | basil |

Extra melted butter for the inside of the pumpkin.
Salt and freshly ground pepper to taste.
*Large enough to easily hold 3 quarts of soup.
**Save the seeds for roasting.

## method

- Brush the inside of the hollowed-out pumpkin with some melted butter, mixed with salt and pepper. Place the pumpkin on a baking pan and bake it in a preheated, 400-degree oven for 20 to 30 minutes.
- In a large stock pot, heat the oil and butter. As it melts, add the onion and sauté it for about 3 minutes. Add the carrots, celery, and 3 cups of the broth. Bring the soup to a boil and add tomatoes. Boil it for about 5 minutes, and then add the rice, remaining broth, and seasoning.
- When the pumpkin is hot, pour the soup into this "Jack-O'-Lantern," and return it to the oven to bake about 60 more minutes, or until the rice is tender.

# Q is for QUINOA SOUP

The **Q family** just loves this dish. Quinoa is not a vegetable, but it does come from a plant.

Have you ever tried quinoa? Or are you asking, "What is quinoa?" LOL. It's ok if you don't know. If you like rice or pasta or grits you may enjoy quinoa! The odd sounding item (pronounced KEEN-wah) is a grain! If you are a vegetarian, then you have most likely already tried it because it is a **great** source of protein!
After you try quinoa, please write me and let me know what you think.

Quinoa grows high in the **Andes Mountains** of **South America** in a place called the **Altiplano**.
   Do you know what that word means?
   Do some research and learn what makes the Altiplano such a special place.

*FOR COMMUNITY SOUP: TWO POUNDS OF QUIONA, COOKED. ADD TWO TABLESPOONS INTO EACH BOWL BEFORE ADDING SOUP.*

## ingredients

| | | |
|---|---|---|
| 4 | tablespoons | butter |
| 2 | large | onions, peeled & diced |
| 5 | cloves | garlic, chopped |
| 1 | large | shallot, peeled & chopped |
| 1½ | cups | quinoa, rinsed well in a sieve |
| 2 | large | yellow potatoes, peeled & diced |
| 2 | cups | water |
| 2 | cups | milk |
| 3 | sprigs | cilantro |
| 1 | teaspoon | turmeric |
| ½ | pounds | peanuts, finely crushed & toasted |
| 2½ | teaspoons | kosher salt |

Salt and freshly ground pepper to taste.

## method

- To a large stock pot, add 3 tablespoons of butter (keep 1 tablespoon of butter for later). Heat the butter until it is melted. Add the onions and garlic, and cook them, stirring occasionally, until the onion is soft—about 10 minutes. Add the last tablespoon of butter and the turmeric, stirring until the butter melted and a beautiful yellow coloration starts to show.
- Add the quinoa, 2 quarts of water, and potatoes to the pot. Cover it and bring the soup to a boil. Reduce the heat to low and allow the soup to simmer for 30 minutes.
- Add the milk, cilantro, salt, pepper, and crushed peanuts. Reduce the heat to very low and let the soup simmer for another 15 minutes. Be careful not to let it burn—keep an eye on it and stir frequently.

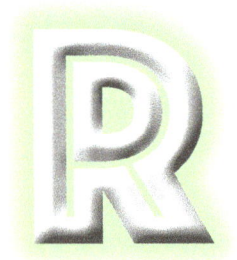

is for

**Mr R.** gets very happy when the wife says, "Dear, what kind of root would you like in the soup tonight?"
He just starts a big rolly polly belly laugh, and is just so happy! Then he starts naming root vegetables.

How many can you name? It's ok to ask your friends.

Speaking of rolly polly bellies and roots...
It's safe to say that I used to be a bigger man than I am now. And that's okay. I'm getting back to my roots...my healthy-eating roots.
Can you guess what I'm eating? Write to me and I will tell you :-)

FOR COMMUNITY SOUP: TWO POUNDS OF RUTABAGAS, PEELED & DICED.

## ingredients

| | | |
|---|---|---|
| 6 | tablespoons | butter |
| 3 | medium | onions, chopped |
| 4 | medium cloves | garlic |
| 2 | small | beets, peeled & diced |
| 4-5 | medium | carrots, peeled & diced |
| 4 | ribs | celery, cut into ½-inch pieces |
| 1 | medium | celery root, peeled & diced |
| 1 | cup | dill, chopped |
| 3 | tablespoons | taragon, chopped |
| 2 | cups | vegetable broth |
| 2 | pounds | ripe heirloom tomatoes, chopped |
| 1 | orange | { orange zest, finely grated / orange juice, freshly squeezed |

Salt and freshly ground pepper to taste.

Sour cream for garnish and cornbread for serving.

## method

- In a large stock pot, melt the butter, add the onion and garlic, and sauté until soft—about 4 minutes.
- Increase the heat to medium-high and add the beets, carrots, celery, celery root, and half the dill. Sauté the vegetables, adjusting heat as needed until they have released their liquid, dried, and start to turn golden color, but not brown—about 20 minutes.
- Add the broth and tomatoes, and bring the soup to a boil. Reduce the heat and continue cooking the soup until the vegetables are soft—about 45 minutes. Add the orange zest and juice, and the remaining dill and tarragon. Season with salt and pepper, to taste. To serve, ladle soup into bowls and top each portion with a dollop of sour cream. Serve with slices of cornbread.

# S is for SUMMER SQUASH SOUP

**Summer Squash** are soft-skinned members of the squash family, such as zucchini, yellow, patty pan, crookneck, and golden zucchini. Remember how happy **Mrs. M** was to make a soup that used a double M? Well, look at the name of the dish **Mrs. S** came up with! I am sure she will be in the running for using the most letters this week!

Way to go, **Mrs. S**! And it's good soup too. You will have to ask your Mom, Dad, or Grandparents to help you make this soup.
My boys, **Curtis Junior** and **Cole,** loved to help me in the kitchen. Here we are, on set, throwing down some moves!

FOR COMMUNITY SOUP: TWO POUNDS OF YELLOW & PATTY PAN SQUASH, CUT INTO ½-INCH PIECES.

## ingredients

| | | |
|---|---|---|
| 1 | tablespoon | vegetable oil |
| 1 | medium | yellow onion, sliced |
| 2 | pounds | summer squash, thinly sliced |
| 1 | cup | coconut milk |
| 3 | cups | vegetable broth |
| 1 | sheet | yuba,* cut into small pieces |
| 1 | teaspoon | fresh ginger, minced |
| 1 | teaspoon | lemongrass, minced |
| 1 | teaspoon | curry powder |
| ½ | cup | cilantro leaves, chopped |

Salt and freshly ground pepper to taste.

*You can substitute ¼-cup finely sliced tofu for yuba.

## method

- In a soup pot, combine the oil, onion, ginger, lemongrass, and a bit of salt. Place the mixture over medium-low heat and sauté it until the onion is tender—about 3 to 4 minutes. Add the curry powder and stir for two more minutes.
- Add the squash, coconut milk, and broth. Season with salt. Cover the pot and simmer the soup until the squash is tender. Allow the soup to cool or lower its temperature by placing the pot in an ice bath. Purée the soup until it is smooth (I love my hand-held blender for puréeing soups).
- Pass the soup through a fine-meshed strainer set over the saucepan and return it to medium-low heat. Add the yuba or tofu and bring soup to a simmer. Remove from heat, add cilantro, and taste to adjust seasoning. Serve and enjoy!

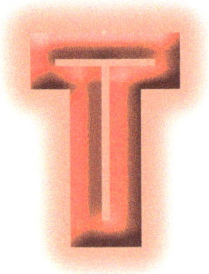

# T is for TOMATO SOUP NORTH AFRICAN STYLE

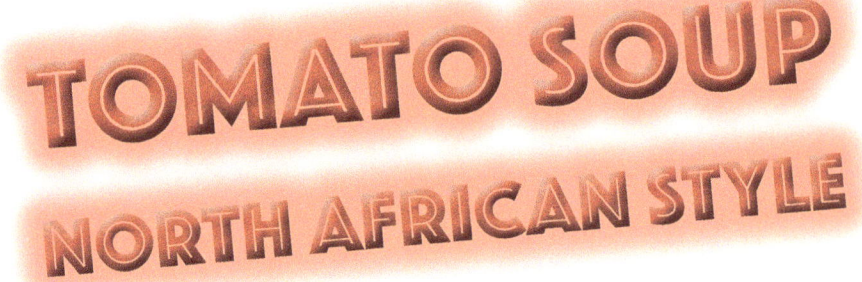

People love coming to the **Family T's** house for dinner, especially late in the summer when all kinds of tomatoes are available. Tonight's soup is from the continent of Africa, and is an old family recipe.

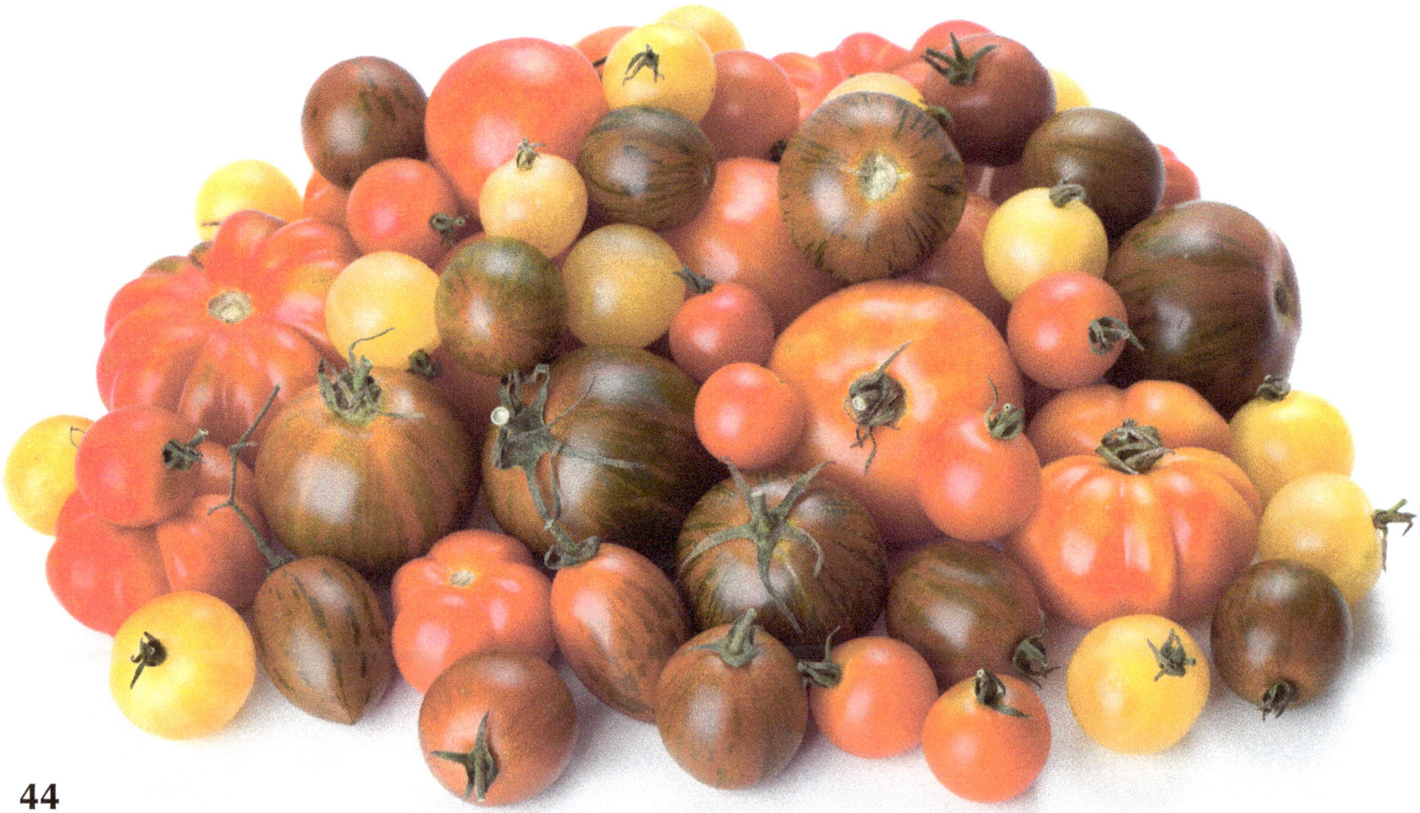

FOR COMMUNITY SOUP: ALL THE INGREDIENTS FOR TOMATO SOUP, PREPPED AND ADDED TO THE COMMUNITY POT. WOW!

## ingredients

| | | |
|---|---|---|
| 6 | cloves | garlic |
| 3 | teaspoons | paprika |
| 2 | teaspoons | cumin, ground |
| ¼ | teaspoon | cayenne pepper |
| 4 | teaspoons | peanut oil |
| 3 | pounds | heirloom tomatoes, cored & diced |
| ½ | cup | cilantro leaves, chopped |
| 1 | tablespoon | apple cider vinegar |
| 2 | tablespoons | fresh lemon juice |
| 4 | stalks | celery, diced |
| 2 | tablespoons | vegetable broth |

Salt and freshly ground pepper to taste.

## method

- In a small saucepan, stir together the garlic, paprika, cumin, cayenne pepper, and olive oil. Place the pan over medium-low heat and cook, stirring constantly, for 5 minutes. Remove the pan from the heat and set it aside.
- Pass the tomatoes through a food mill fitted with a large disk (if you don't have a food mill, then chop the tomatoes as fine as you can and push through a strainer, or use your hand-held blender to blend them before running them through the strainer).
- Add the cooked spice, cilantro, vinegar, lemon juice, salt, celery, and vegetable broth. Taste and add pepper and salt, if needed. Chill before serving.

**Do you know where Africa is? Do you know how many continents there are?**

 is for **UPLAND CRESS SOUP & CAVIAR**

Upland Cress is a delicate leafy green, with a slightly peppery taste, that is great to add to salads and sandwiches. However, the unassuming and upstanding **Family U** loves to use this vegetable to make soup!

*If I can talk you kids into trying this recipe, I think you may be surprised how good it is.*

And, speaking of caviar, one of my caviar moments in life was meeting **First Lady Michelle Obama!** **WOW!**
I got to meet her when I went to the **White House** to cook in her **Kids and Chefs** program with the Georgia state winners of **The Healthy Lunchtime Challenge.**
—Hi, Mira and Corey!

FOR COMMUNITY SOUP: THREE POUNDS OF UPLAND CRESS, DIVIDED AND PLACED INTO EACH BOWL BEFORE THE SOUP IS ADDED.

## ingredients

| | | |
|---|---|---|
| 3 | tablespoons | butter, unsalted |
| 1 | pound | leeks,* halved & thinly sliced |
| 1 | large | onion, peeled & finely chopped |
| 4 | cups | vegetable broth |
| 3 | cups | heavy cream |
| 3 | bunches | cress,** rinsed & stems removed |
| 1 | | lemon, juiced |
| 2 | tablespoons | caviar |

Sea salt and freshly ground white pepper to taste.

*Wash leeks well and use only the white and light green portions.

**Blanched for about 3 minutes, shocked in ice water, then puréed and strained. Discard the strained water.

## method

- Melt the butter in a large stockpot over medium heat. Stir in the leeks, onion, and salt. Cover and cook over low heat until the vegetables are soft—about 4 minutes.
- Add broth and 2 cups of the cream, then raise the heat to medium-high and bring the soup to a gentle boil. Simmer the soup, on low and uncovered, for 30 minutes.
- Purée the soup and return the mixture to the stockpot over medium-high heat. Bring it to a gentle boil and, using a slotted spoon, skim off the foam that rises to the surface. Allow soup to cool.
- To serve, reheat the soup. Meanwhile, using an electric mixer, whip the remaining cup of cream to stiff peaks (you know how to take a short cut, right? You can do this by hand, but it takes forever).
- Into the warm soup, stir the fresh lemon juice. Season to taste with salt and white pepper. Now, add the watercress purée to the warmed soup and stir in. Place a scoop of whipped cream in the center of each bowl and top with a small spoonful of caviar. Enjoy!

# V is for VEGETABLE CHILI

Certain families in the Alphabet Community, because their names are so versatile, such as **A**, have a wide choice of what to fix at mealtimes. However, in the case of **Family V**, any dinner dish can be called Vegetable Soup, which allows **Mrs. V** to use any vegetable she feels like cooking.

Way to go, **Mrs. V!** What do you think of that? Is it fair to be so versatile?

FOR COMMUNITY SOUP: THREE POUNDS OF MIXED VEGETABLES: CELERY ROOT AND PARSNIP (PEELED AND DICED), AND CELERY IN ½-INCH PIECES.

## ingredients

| 3 | tablespoons | oil |
| 1 | large | onion, peeled & chopped |
| 2 | cloves | garlic, chopped |
| 1 | cup | mushrooms, thinly sliced |
| 1 | | green pepper, chopped |
| 4 | cups | kidney beans |
| 8 | | ripe tomatoes, chopped |
| 4 | ounces | tomato paste |
| 3 | tablespoons | chili powder |

Salt and freshly ground pepper to taste.

## method

- In a large pot, heat the oil. Add the onion and sauté until it starts to brown—about 7 minutes. Add the garlic and cook about 2 minutes. Add the mushrooms, stir, and cook until they start to soften, but be careful not to let them burn.
- Keep some of the vegetable broth nearby; if the food starts to dry out, add a bit of broth. Add the beans, tomatoes, tomato paste, and chili power. Stir them together, replace the pot lid, and bring the chili to a boil. Lower the heat and allow the chili to simmer for about 40 to 50 minutes.

#  is for WINTER SQUASH & WHITE BEAN SOUP

Winter squash is also known as the hard-headed, thick-skinned squash. In this group are **Acorn**, **Hubert**, **Butternut**, **Buttercup**, **Spaghetti**, and the good, old **Pumpkin**!

Question...have you cooked any of the hard-headed squashes? **Mrs. W** has, and she's really good at cooking them! That's because she practices, and you should too. No matter what you do, or want to do, the best way to improve is to **practice**. When I **coached basketball** at **Dominican University** (bet you didn't expect me to be a chef and a coach, did you?), I would tell my players, **"You have to think like a champ to be a champ!"**

And now I saying that to **you** too.

FOR COMMUNITY SOUP: TWO POUNDS OF MIXED WINTER SQUASH, PEELED & DICED INTO ½-INCH PIECES, WHICH CAN BE ROASTED WITH THE YAMS.

## ingredients

| | | |
|---|---|---|
| 1 | pound | white beans, presoaked or canned |
| 2 | tablespoons | oil |
| 1 | medium | onion, chopped |
| 4 | cloves | garlic, minced |
| 2 | quarts | vegetable broth |
| 2 | | leeks,* washed & chopped |
| 1 | pound | winter squash,** peeled & diced |

Salt and freshly ground pepper to taste.

A bouquet garni made with a couple of sprigs each of parsley and thyme, a bay leaf, and 2 sage leaves.

*Wash leeks well and use only the white and light green portions.
**Save the seeds for roasting.

## method

- Heat 1 tablespoon of the oil in a large, heavy soup pot over medium heat and add the onion. Cook it gently until tender—about 5 minutes, and add 2 of the garlic cloves and ½ teaspoon of salt.
- Stir the onion and garlic together for about 30 seconds, and then add the beans and broth. Bring the broth to a boil and skim off foam. Add the bouquet garni, reduce the heat, and cover the pot, allowing the broth to simmer for 1 hour.
- Heat the remaining olive oil in a wide, heavy skillet over medium heat and add the leeks and ½ teaspoon salt. Cook the leeks gently, while stirring, until they are tender—about 3 minutes—and then add the remaining garlic and the squash.
- Cook the soup, while stirring, until the garlic makes the kitchen smells like Gilroy (A city in California that is famous for its garlic farms...it smells good), and the squash is coated with oil and just beginning to soften—about 2 minutes.
- Remove the soup from heat and stir it into the beans. Add salt, to taste, and continue to simmer for another 30 minutes to an hour, or until the beans and vegetables are thoroughly tender and falling apart. Taste the soup, adjust the amount of salt, and remove the bouquet garni.
- You can serve the soup chunky or purée it for a smooth, cream-like soup. If you purée the soup, float a drizzle of olive oil on top.

# X is for HUGS (& KISSES) TO BLESS (& COOL) THE SOUP

Because there are no vegetables that begin with X, the **Family X** uses love. At the **COMMUNITY DINNER,** they are in charge of cooling down the dish so every family can enjoy their meal. X and O, hugs and kisses, combine to represent love, and love is so important. XO, XO is like giving hugs and blowing kisses, so the **X's** and **O's** get together in a big hug around the big stock pot, and it is such a lovely sight! Then, other families join in to cool the hot pot before serving the soup!

I like this saying: **1** is strong on its own, but with **2**, what could we do? Add **3** and **4**, to truly open the door.

What would you do if one of your friends and their family had nothing to make for dinner? I need your help, and the **Family X** needs your help. I want you to tell me how we can help feed this family in our Alphabet Community. Please write to me with your suggestions of how to help hungry families. **Spread love.**

Now, remember—early in the book—when I talked about friends, and that right inside of you, you have a friend? That friend is **you!** I don't mean that you have to be your only friend; however, it is good to know yourself, right? You have to take care of yourself so you can help care for others. Learn to read, so you can teach yourself. Remember, I didn't learn to read until I was 26-years old. Wow, right?

It was so difficult, some days, going to school, worried that my friends would find out I could not read. Now, I can read, and—wow!—it's like the brightest lights are on and I can see everything! When I was your age, I used speaking to help cover up that I couldn't read. And I still love talking! To individuals and groups—little, big, the larger the better. I love it. I try to shine.

**And I want you to shine too!**

 is for

Tell the truth, have you ever heard of making soup from **Yams?** Okay, don't judge it until you've tried it. In many of the developing parts of the world, yams are among the first food crops established. Any guesses as to why?

Yes, they taste good, but that's not the only reason. Yams are loaded with vitamins A, B, and C, plus all kinds of other Good Stuff your body needs to Grow and Go on.

This is why **Mrs. Y** loves serving her family the incredible, edible Yam!

Speaking of truth, did you know that the vegetable that we call a yam in the United States is actually a **Sweet Potato?**

What do you think of that?

I found this cool sculpture at the Bass Museum of Art in Miami Beach, Florida.
My question to you reminded me of it: the question of real and fake. In a way, I wasn't totally real when I was in school because I never told anyone that I couldn't read.
I don't want any of you to have to go through that...if you struggle with reading, tell a parent, grandparent, or a teacher. They can help you.

FOR COMMUNITY SOUP: TWO POUNDS OF YAMS PEELED AND DICED INTO CUBES ABOUT ½-INCH EACH. ROAST 30 MINUTES WITH A LITTLE OIL AT 400.

## ingredients

| | | |
|---|---|---|
| 2 | pounds | yams, peeled & cubed (1-inch) |
| 1 | large | red onion, chopped |
| 1 | clove | garlic, finely chopped |
| 3 | large | carrots, coarsely chopped |
| 1 | stalk | celery, coarsely chopped |
| 2 | quarts | light vegetable broth |
| ½ | teaspoon | salt |
| 1 | teaspoon | pepper, freshly ground |
| 1 | tablespoon | thyme leaves, fresh |
| 6 | tablespoons | yogurt, plain low-fat |
| 6 | sprigs | parsley, no stems, finely chopped |
| 1 | | bay leaf |

## method

- Put the yams, onion, garlic, carrots, celery, bay leaf, thyme, and vegetable broth into a large pot. Bring the soup to a boil over medium-high heat. Lower the heat and simmer the soup until the yams are tender—about 30 minutes.
- Check seasoning by tasting, and add pepper, if need be. Ladle the soup into bowls and garnish with dollops of yogurt and chopped parsley.
- For a different style of soup, purée the vegetables and broth in a blender until it is smooth. Pass the soup through a sieve. Continue to purée and strain until all of the vegetables and broth have been puréed, and then serve it up and garnish it with yogurt and parsley.

# Z is for ZUCCHINI & HERB SOUP

The **Family Z** loves **Zucchini**, especially the kids. And **Mom Z** isn't really sure if it's because she is a great zucchini cook or if the little ones just love the sound they make when they say, "ZUCCHINI!"

Are there any foods that you love to eat for reasons other than how they taste?

For me it's **Brussel Sprouts**. Want to know why?

Because I don't like their taste; but I still eat them.

That's right, I eat the untasty (to me) vegetable at least two times a year, just in case I find that I have come to like them! LOL

Don't be afraid to try something *different* or to BE different!

FOR COMMUNITY SOUP: TWO POUNDS OF ZUCCHINI, CUT INTO ½-INCH PIECES.

## ingredients

| 2 | pounds | zucchini, trimmed and cut |
| 1 | large | onion, chopped |
| 2 | cloves | garlic, chopped |
| ¼ | cup | olive oil |
| 4 | cups | light vegetable broth, divided |
| ¼ | cup | fresh tarragon |
| ¼ | cup | fresh dill |
| ½ | cup | basil leaves |

## method

- In a heavy stock pot, cook the onion and garlic in oil over medium-low heat, stirring occasionally, until they are softened or about 5 minutes.
- Add the chopped zucchini and 1 teaspoon of salt, and cook, stirring occasionally, for 4 minutes. Add 3 cups of the vegetable broth, and then simmer, partially covered, until the zucchini is tender—about 20 minutes.
- Add the herbs and cook the soup about 2 minutes more. Purée the soup with a pitcher-style blender in 2 batches or with a hand-held stick blender.
- Garnish the soup with finely chopped red onion and tomatoes.

# COMMUNITY SOUP

The ABC community gathers every month at the Alphabet Center, where they discuss ways of making life in and around their neighborhood better, all the Moms and Dads, and even the kids, join in the conversation. The highlight, after all the hellos and hugs and business talk, is making the community soup. The kitchen at the Center is well stocked with the staples needed for cooking, as well as pots, pans, and all the utensils. The staples are items such as salt, pepper, and other seasonings and dry herbs, plus vegetable broth.

The families take turns setting up the kitchen for soup time. This month it happens to be **Family A**, so they have brought out the big stock pot, the seasonings, different vegetable oils—corn, olive, and walnut—and vegetable broth; everything is out and ready to go. All that is left to do now is to add the ingredients to the pot and let the magic happen!

## Community soup

### Ingredients, by the letters...

- 1 pound of asparagus, green or purple, cut into 1-inch pieces
- 1 pound of broccoli florets, trimmed
- 1 to 2 bunches of celery, washed and cut into about 1-inch pieces
- 2 pounds of daikon, peeled and cut into ½-inch pieces
- 7 cloves of elephant garlic, peeled and crushed

3 cups of fava beans, use same prep as for family soup

3 tablespoons of ginger, peeled and chopped

Double batch of horseradish sauce

2 cups of fresh Indian peas

3 medium jicama, peeled and diced

4 kohlrabi, peeled and diced

4 pounds of lemon cucumber, diced; ½-teaspoon in each bowl before soup

1 ounce of dried porcini mushrooms

1 pound of fresh Morel mushroom; see **M** soup for prep instructions

1 tablespoon of nutmeg

3 pounds of Vidalia onions, chopped; sauté in oil until they are translucent

½ pound of hot peppers, washed and cut, on the side for those who want it

2 pounds of quinoa, precooked; add 2 tablespoon to each bowl, as desired

2 pounds of rutabagas, peeled and diced

2 pounds of yellow and patty pan squash, cut into ½-inch pieces

3 pounds of heirloom tomatoes, cored and cut into 1-inch pieces

3 pounds of upland cress; add cress to each bowl before soup, as desired

3 pounds of mixed vegetables: celery and okra, cut into ½-inch pieces; celery root and parsnip, peeled and diced

2 pounds of mixed winter squash: acorn and butternut, peeled and diced; for added flavor these can be roasted before adding to the soup

**X** is bringing the **LOVE**

2 pounds of yams, peeled and diced; roast before adding to the soup

2 pounds zucchini cut into ½-inch pieces

## Method

- To the large stock pot, add about ½ cup of oil and heat. The ingredients that are optional—those that are added to each serving—are placed to the side:
  - Set to the side the horseradish sauce
  - Place ½ teaspoon of lemon cucumber into each bowl
  - Make available the cut hot peppers for anyone that wants to add heat
  - Place a small bunch of upland cress into each bowl
  - Place 2 tablespoons of precooked quinoa into each bowl (more if desired)

**Let's make our soup!**

- Families with the vegetables that require a longer cooking time bring theirs early, to add to the hot oil.
- Sauté the celery and daikon for about 3 minutes, add the jicama, kohlrabi, and half the elephant garlic; sauté 3 more minutes. The house smells GOOD!
- Add the Vidalia onion, sauté just a bit longer, about 1 to 2 minutes.
- Add about ½ cup of vegetable broth. Allow to cook about 3 minutes.
- Now add to pot all the remaining vegetables, including all those brought by the **Family V**. Okra is one of the keys, because that vegetable will help to thicken our soup.
- Once all the vegetables are in the pot, add enough of the vegetable broth to cover everything, and bring the soup to a boil.
- Lower the heat, and then allow the soup to simmer about 20 to 40 minutes.
- Adjust the seasoning by adding pepper and a little salt, if needed.
- Serve up with any of the optional add-ins and a dollop of sour cream.
- Enjoy your ABC soup!

# One last thing...

So have you figured out what the word metaphor means? Well, it's when someone compares stuff without using the words "like" or "as" (because that would be a simile). Is my statement about best friends and the ABCs a metaphor?

Here is an example of a metaphor:

In the morning, my teacher is a lion!

Oh, my! Fortunately:

But, by the time school is out, she is a kitten.

## Photo and Art Credits

|  | SOURCE | CREDIT |
|---|---|---|
| Front Cover | Prospective Press | ARTE RAVE |
|  | Dollar Photo Club | Kurhan |
|  |  | Oleh Tokarev |
|  |  | Prawny |
|  |  | Seamartini Graphics |
| Back Cover | Prospective Press | ARTE RAVE |
| v | Curtis Aikens | Photographer Unknown |
| vi |  | Suze Gorman |
| 4 |  | Photographer Unknown |
| 6 | Dollar Photo Club | Picture Partners |
| 7 | Curtis Aikens | Curtis Aikens |
| 8 |  | White House Photographer |
| 9 | Dollar Photo Club | Africa Studio |
| 11 |  | zahar2000 |
| 12 | Curtis Aikens | Curtis Aikens |
| inset 13 |  |  |
| 13 | Dollar Photo Club | sasimoto |
| 15 | Curtis Aikens | Curtis Aikens |
| 16 |  | Photographer Unknown |
| 17 |  | Curtis Aikens |
| 18 | Morgue File | kamuelaboy |
| 19 | Curtis Aikens | Curtis Aikens |
| 21 |  | Photographer Unknown |
| photo 22 |  |  |
| frame 23 | Prospective Press | ARTE RAVE |
| 23 | Dollar Photo Club | drevalyusha |
| 24 | Curtis Aikens | Curtis Aikens |
| 25 |  |  |
| 26 | Dollar Photo Club | tpzijl |
| 27 |  | st-fotograf |

## Photo and Art Credits

| | SOURCE | CREDIT |
|---|---|---|
| 28 | Curtis Aikens | Photographer Unknown |
| 29 | Dollar Photo Club | Marek |
| 31 | | bendicks |
| 32 | Curtis Aikens | Photographer Unknown |
| 33 | Dollar Photo Club | tpzijl |
| 34 | Curtis Aikens | Photographers Unknown |
| 35 | | Curtis Aikens |
| 36 | | Photographer Unknown |
| 37 | Dollar Photo Club | Gorilla |
| 38 | | Valentin Valkov |
| 39 | | shantihesse |
| 40 | Curtis Aikens | Photographer Unknown |
| photos 2 & 3 40 | | Curtis Aikens |
| 41 | | |
| 42 | | Photographer Unknown |
| 43 | Dollar Photo Club | MSPhotographic |
| 44 | | Pavlo Kucherov |
| 45 | | JMC |
| 46 | Curtis Aikens | White House Photographer |
| 47 | | Curtis Aikens |
| all 48 | | |
| 49 | Dollar Photo Club | Rony Zmiri |
| photo 50 | Curtis Aikens | Photographer Unknown |
| frame 50 | Prospective Press | ARTE RAVE |
| 51 | Dollar Photo Club | xixinxing |
| 53 | | Malyshchyts Viktar |
| 54 | Curtis Aikens | Curtis Aikens |
| 55 | Dollar Photo Club | sasazawa |
| turnouts 56 | Curtis Aikens | Photographer Unknown |
| shoes 56 | | Curtis Aikens |
| 57 | Dollar Photo Club | famveldman |
| 61 | | Malyshchyts Viktar |

www.ingramcontent.com/pod-product-compliance
Lightning Source LLC
Chambersburg PA
CBHW051254110526
44588CB00026B/2989